Norman Nawrocki
No Masters! No Gods!

Also by Norman Nawrocki

Cazzarola! Anarchy, Romani, Love, Italy
Red: Quebec student strike and social revolt poems
Nightcap for Nihilists
Dinner for Dissidents
Lunch for Insurgents
Breakfast for Anarchists
The Anarchist & The Devil Do Cabaret
Chasseur de Tornades
Rebel Moon: @narchist rants & poems
Resist Much - Obey Little
Rhythm Activism Live

Norman Nawrocki
No Masters! No Gods!

Dare to dream

Illustrations by Philtre

LES PAGES NOIRES

MONTREAL

No Masters! No Gods! Dare to dream

This new and revised edition
published in 2015 by Les Pages Noires,
Montreal, Quebec, Canada
LPN026B

rhythm@nothingness.org
www.nothingness.org/music/rhythm

First published in 1999
by SMARTEN UP! & Get To The Point Publishing,
Vancouver, BC, Canada.
Copyright © 1999 Norman Nawrocki
Illustrations: Copyright © 2015 Philippe Caron

All rights reserved. No part of this book may be reproduced,
saved in a retrieval system, or transmitted by any form in any part
or by any means without written permission from the publisher,
except by a reviewer, who may use brief excerpts in a review.

Printed and bound in Canada by Marquis
on FSC eco-friendly, recycled paper

ISBN 978-2-9805763-6-2
Canadian Cataloguing in Publication Data:
Nawrocki, Norman
No Masters! No Gods! Dare to dream

Dépôt légal – Bibliothèque et Archives nationales du Québec, 2015
Dépôt légal – Library and Archives Canada, 2015

Cover art, graphic design and production: Philippe Caron
Distributed in Canada by Les Pages Noires Distribution
Distributed in USA & Europe by AK Press   www.akpress.org

7	A son from the East End
11	Neo-Neanderthals
13	No one knows
15	Suitable squeegee punks
18	No more walls
19	Hey garcon!
23	Power talk
26	The Velorution is coming!
29	How to support a worthy cause
32	A Wobbly dinner
34	The hacker
36	Mutiny
38	Grandma's request
40	Tin can alley
43	Think revolution
47	Heterosexual Reinforcement Pill
48	Dry love
50	I want to make a citizen's arrest
53	Tears are true
55	She walks with a cane
57	Montreal! You've got no heart, no art

A SON FROM THE EAST END

I am a son from the East End
of Vancouver, Edmonton, Winnipeg,
Toronto, Hamilton, Montreal and Halifax
beside the tracks
the neighbourhood of tightly spaced,
cracked houses, tight jeans, tight-lipped,
unsteady with the tongue
who use soap to wash away
truths stamped into skin
sometimes taut around the ribs
but never as 'white' as yours

I am a son from the East End
kitchens painted over and over peeling yellow
filled with spirits from the old country
whose voices laced with curry, dill, garlic,
lime, chili, ginger and onions
seep through thin walls
into crooked stairwells and dank corners
where cultures clash and retreat
behind double-locked doors and grills
you sell to keep us apart

I am a son from the East End
schools overcrowded, underfunded
career trade streamlined
where we learn to speak your language
because ours has no place
learn your history
because ours does not exist
to follow your goose-stepping get ahead footsteps
because ours, we are told, lead nowhere
to bow before your Gods and rich white guys
because we have no heroes
except yours

I am a son from the East End
streets where cruising cops
teach us respect for your laws 'n orders
and how they can kick ass on night shifts
when no one is around
except us, the restless, and them, the guards
because you pay, arm and instruct them
to watch us, stop us, harass us, beat us
keep us away from your gold-plated gates
how they tempt us

I am a son from the East End
who tried to understand your ways
dress like you, smell like you
talk and walk like you
remember everything you told me
find the money you said was all mine
realize the two-bit dream you spelled out for me
live my life following your rules
mouth shut bite my tongue yes sir
to keep things the way they were
until the day I finally
woke up and said
Fuck you
I am a son of the East End
Get out of my way

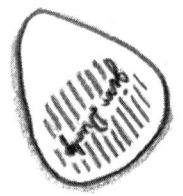

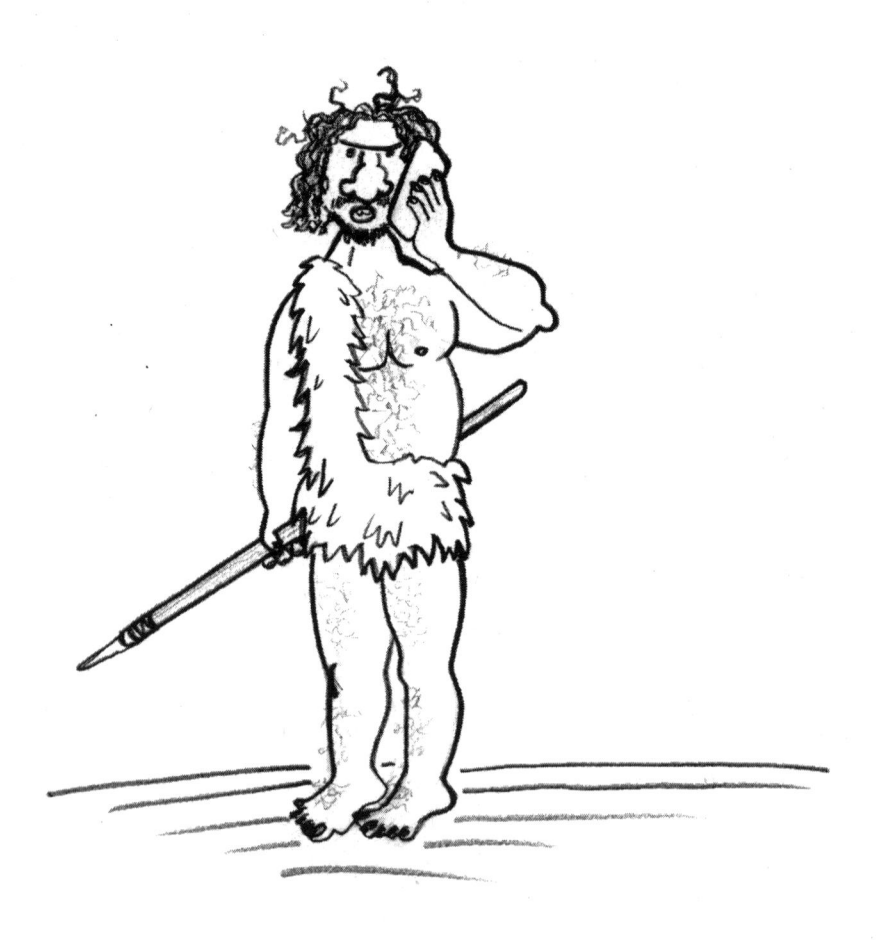

NEO-NEANDERTHALS

From out of the cave
a recycled, glorified, used car salesman
beating his chest
'The best, the best of all con men!'
All hail might, mighty, Neanderthal Man
Primitive accumulation his historic last stand
gathering more sticks and stones
his brilliant life plan
'For one and all, children too!'
Primitive accumulation his retreaded, retooled God
All hail mighty, mighty, Neanderthal Man
sitting on the biggest pile of shit
his brain clogged with primitive greed and rot
this self-proclaimed, mealy-mouthed saviour
who vomits and talks non-stop
Al hail mighty, mighty Neanderthal Man
'Humour me, tolerate me, listen to me!'
Listen to the birds, the crickets, the wind:
History only forgives if we give it a while
but we don't have much time left -
ask the planet
each one of us, only one life to bet
Yet mighty, mighty Neanderthal Man calls the shots
with his primitive accumulation
suit and tie and head full of rocks
All hail the 21st century corporate warrior
dodo bird
All hail mighty, mighty Neanderthal Man
'The best, the best of all con men!'

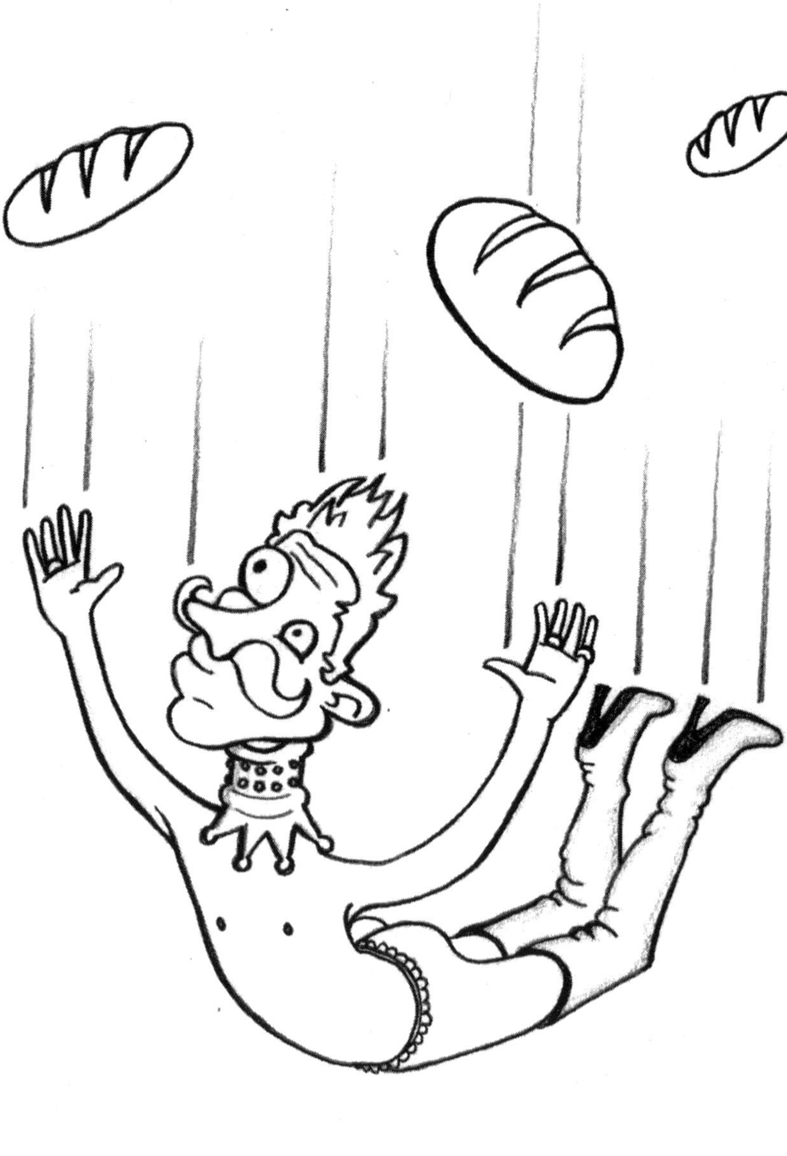

NO ONE KNOWS

No one knows the length of the rope
the curve of the loaf
the goat in the boat
who's going to float
the weight of time
who fathers the future
No one knows

No one knows
the age of prosperity
the mother of gravity
the knight in the moon
the drift of the crow
the strength of the goose
whether ducks can row
No one knows

    But the King is dead!
    The Queen is dead!
    Rise with the bread!
    Rise with the bread!
    The King is dead!
    The Queen is dead!
    Rise with the bread!
    Rise with the bread!

No one knows the square of the plumb
the rate of submission
the tone of the kettle
the ring of attrition
which half the calf
which road the toad
No one knows

No one knows
do mice take ice
does the Pope have lice
the colour of time
from where comes the rhyme
how white is light
how black the night
No one knows

    But the King is dead!
    The Queen is dead!
    Rise with the bread!
    Rise with the bread!
    The King is dead!
    The Queen is dead!
    Rise with the bread!
    Rise with the bread!

SUITABLE SQUEEGEE PUNKS

I'm fed up with seeing squeegee punks
dart in and out of traffic
pretending to earn a living
I'm sick and tired of seeing squeegee punks
risk life and limb for a bit of spare change
a finger and a glare
I'm sick and tired of seeing squeegee punks
chased out of city after city
harassed and beaten by cops
criminalized for trying to stay alive
Instead, give me some squeegee suits –
over-fed, whiskey drunk, power hungry rich men –
I wanna see squeegee free marketeers from the
Stock Market forced to dumpster dive
for their daily stale bread
I wanna see squeegee corporate lawyers
dart in and out of traffic for some bad mouthing
and maybe a looney
I wanna see squeegee city councillors
duck and hide every time they see a police car
I wanna see squeegee right wing radio talk show hosts
wipe the snot from their noses on their sleeves
as they try to find a dry place under a bridge to sleep
I wanna see squeegee politicians and businessmen
the ones who force people to beg and scrounge in the streets
so they and their friends can live carefree, smug and secure
behind their cutbacks and layoffs, their dismantling
of social safety nets, their attacks on the poor
I wanna see them shiver in the rain
and feel like pieces of shit
for just trying to feed themselves
Because each and every one of them
all those self-righteous upholders
of law and their created disorder
all those corporate rip-off artists
who plunder this country
and rob the people

all those untouchable CEOs who owe millions in deferred taxes
yet own $50 million, 12 seater corporate commuter jets
all those who hide their uncounted wealth in offshore banks
but clamour for more government handouts
while they lay off thousands
all those who rail against squeegee punks
welfare mothers and the unemployed
then blame the poor
so the heat is off them and their thieving ways

I wanna see all those assholes held accountable
and charged with theft, disturbing the peace
endangering our lives
and that of the planet
I wanna see all of them lined up against a wall
squeegees held high in their hands at attention
as we, the People, sentence them to a lifetime of
keeping everyone's windshields and windows bug-free
our vision clear
because you know what?
I'm sick and tired of seeing squeegee punks
dart in and out of traffic
pretending to earn a living.

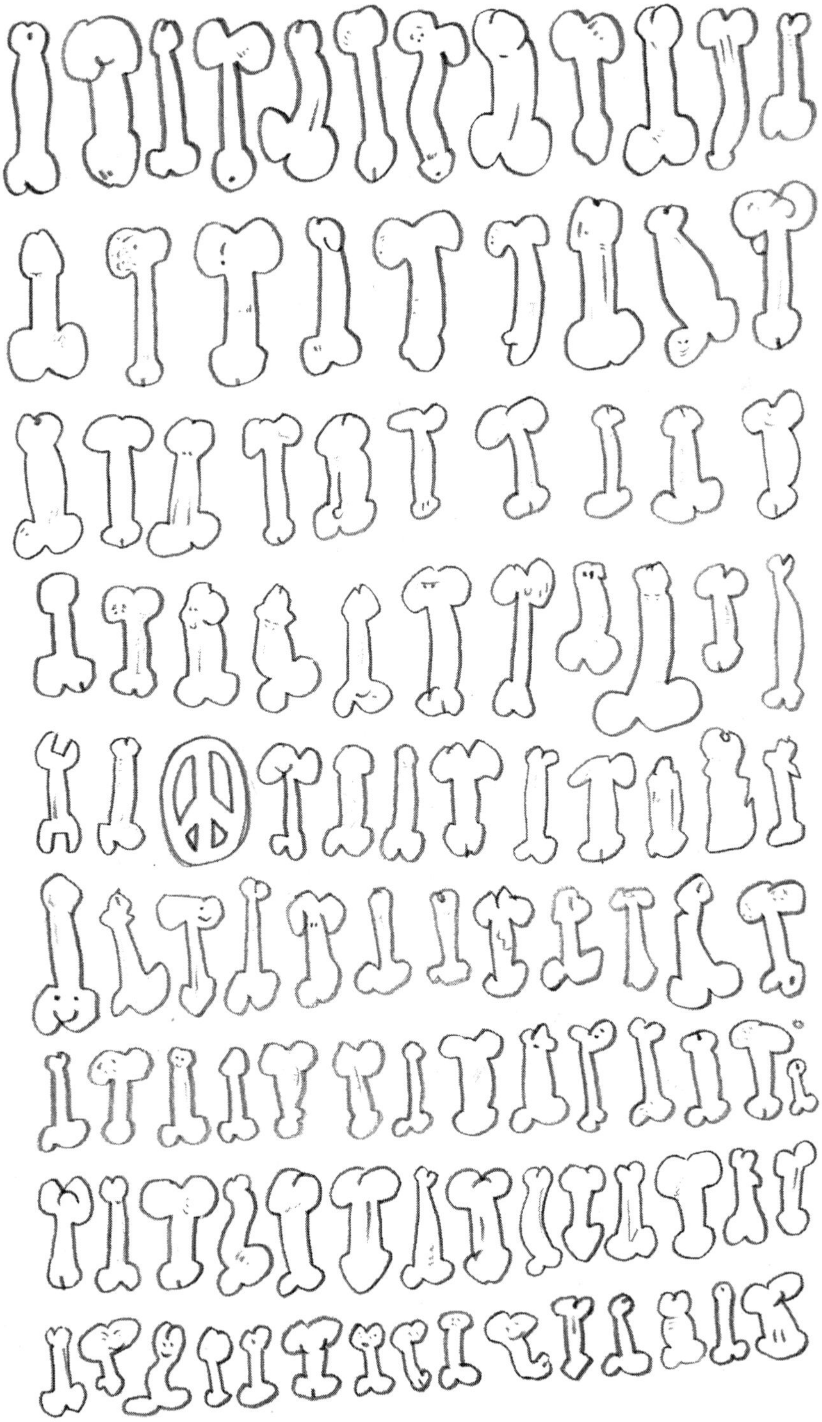

NO MORE WALLS

Are you a 'straight man' who suffers minor anxiety attacks
every time you sit on public transit beside a male stranger?
Do you sweat a little thinking,
'Oh, oh, better not get too close
in case he assumes I'm gay or bisexual,
or maybe he's gay or bi-sexual or trans'?
Do you make that extra effort
to stiffen your back, lean the other way,
avoid grazing knees, trying to be more 'manly' or 'straighter,'
hoping he'll get the message and reciprocate?
Do you fear the consequences if you don't make this clear?
If so, then you could be suffering from an emotionally crippling
body odour: HMS - Hyper Masculine Stink - the disease
that sets off an 'anti-homosexual panic attack' and makes you
think irrational thoughts and feel totally insecure.
If you suffer from HMS, then you need a proven antidote:
'NO MORE WALLS BODY SPRAY.'
This amazing, refreshing new body spray helps rid you
of that uber he-man, 'get-away-from-me!'
defensive wall body odour,
and allows you to relax, feel confident, reassured and yourself
around strange men, or women transitioning into men.
Combats tough guy body odour that paralyses you emotionally
and keeps others away.
Tests prove, the same knee-jerk reaction that stops men
from getting close to other men - physically and emotionally -
also works against getting close to women.
With 'NO MORE WALLS BODY SPRAY,'
you can open up and get close instantly -
without necessarily being sexual -
to both men and women.
One whiff of the new you and everyone will think:
'Gee! This guy is so cool! Let's buy him a beer!'
So say good-bye to that old hyper-masculine stink.
Use 'NO MORE WALLS BODY SPRAY' - and smell better.
Available in three manly scents:
New Spice, Spice Dog and Spice Dude.

HEY GARCON! ANOTHER HOT DOG! RIGHT HERE!

How many buffoons
with or without a moustache
does it take to remind the World
that 'leaders' can only 'lead' if we allow them
to lead ourselves into War or a Police State
or a pseudo-referendum or a campaign of race hatred
or the delusion that yet another arrogant suit and tie man,
another well-fed, debt fearing,
company-licking, good-for-nothing, scary lying rich man
knows what's best for you and me
and what's left of this country?
This man does more damage with one champagne belch
than any pissed off kid high
and loose in a mall with a shotgun
This man woos Wall Street with promises of
your Mom's sweat, your Dad's tears, your future – in chains
at Burger King, in servitude, a whole nation
of happy hamburger flippers on call 24/7
tarred and striped forever
This man won't hesitate to turn forests into ass-wipe
fish into sludge, lakes and rivers into imported flush
for thirsty American toilets
This man will trade an army of Lotto losers
for a Virtual Reality Crown
his own evasive shadow for a hit music video
This man ignores drum-pounding Cree, Innu and Mohawk
outside his own fucking door saying
'Hold it buddy'
He can't hear the repeated thud thud thud
of provincial police clubs on red skin
beside lonely darkened highways – the moon don't talk
He can't hear the laughter of underground transit cops
as they boot one more black man
one more homeless punk
one more screaming Latino down concrete stairs
into their office for some fun

This man never hears the chattering of bad teeth
outside bank machines on city streets begging
'spare me, or this land but please spare something'
And you can bet your last, boot-soiled *fleurs-de-lys* or maple leaf
this man does not hear the patriotic flap-flapping
of faded 'A LOUER/FOR RENT' signs
decorating prime Montreal real estate empty and wondering
Who wants it? Wal Mart? Walt Disney?
Walt Whitman Winnebago's Incorporated?
No, all this man hears is canned applause for his speeches
the mantra of his own pocket calculator unbalancing
and the wind blowing through the hole in his head
west down the 401
This man is another bad rerun, and who needs him?
To hell with new nation states, new transnational
banana-flake republix
Los Tabernacos, we the people, nous le peuple
are tired of the con game, the rip offs
and con men, bankers and businessmen
tired of your high-priced circuses you call 'consensus'
You want consensus?
Ask the kids on welfare next door how to live off weekly specials
Do they stretch the soup with water or just eat once a day?
Do they steal other lunches at school?
Sell themselves for a meal?
Now ask their mom how she can live with herself
Don't look at your Rolex or your manicure
Go stuff your dead-handed, flag waving corpse of nationalism
down your own dry throat
then read the spray-paint on the wall:
'The only solution to national dissolution is Social Revolution'
Now give me a flaming poutine, dude
Your limo is leaking gasoline

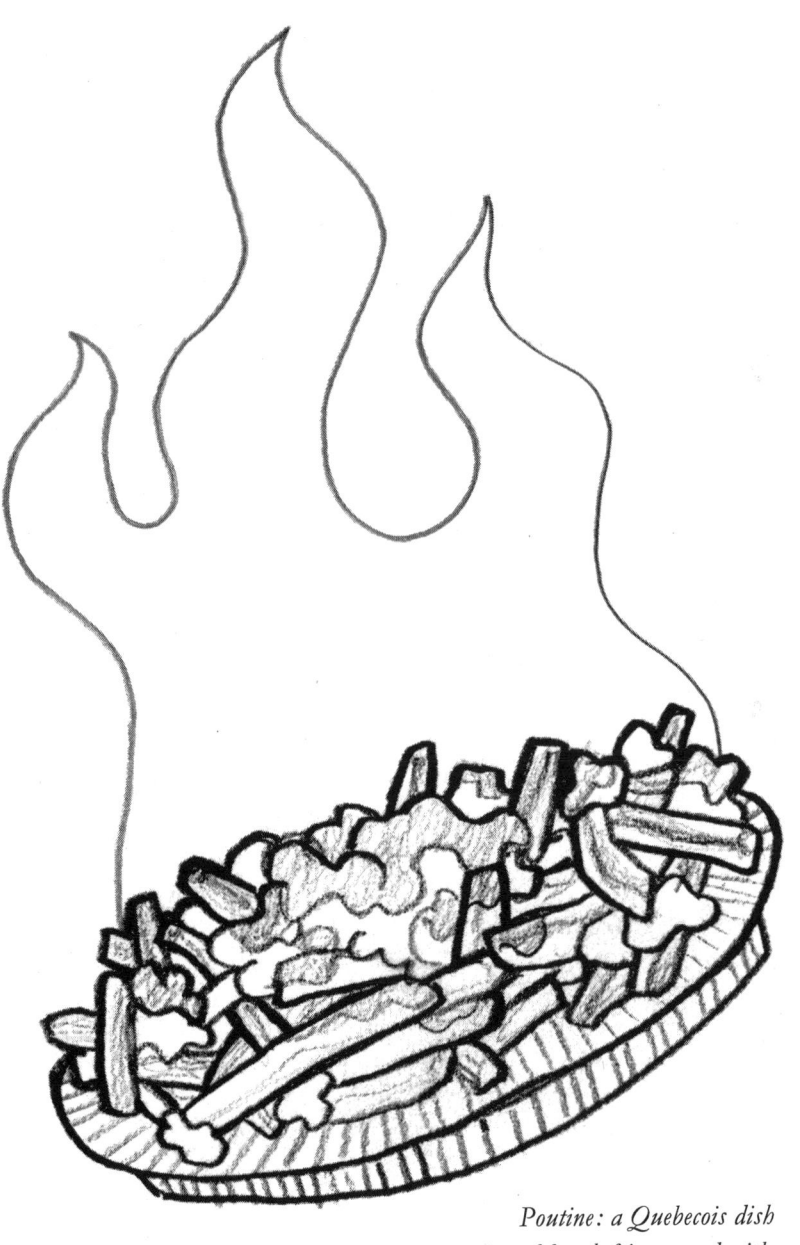

Poutine: a Quebecois dish of french fries topped with cheese curds and gravy

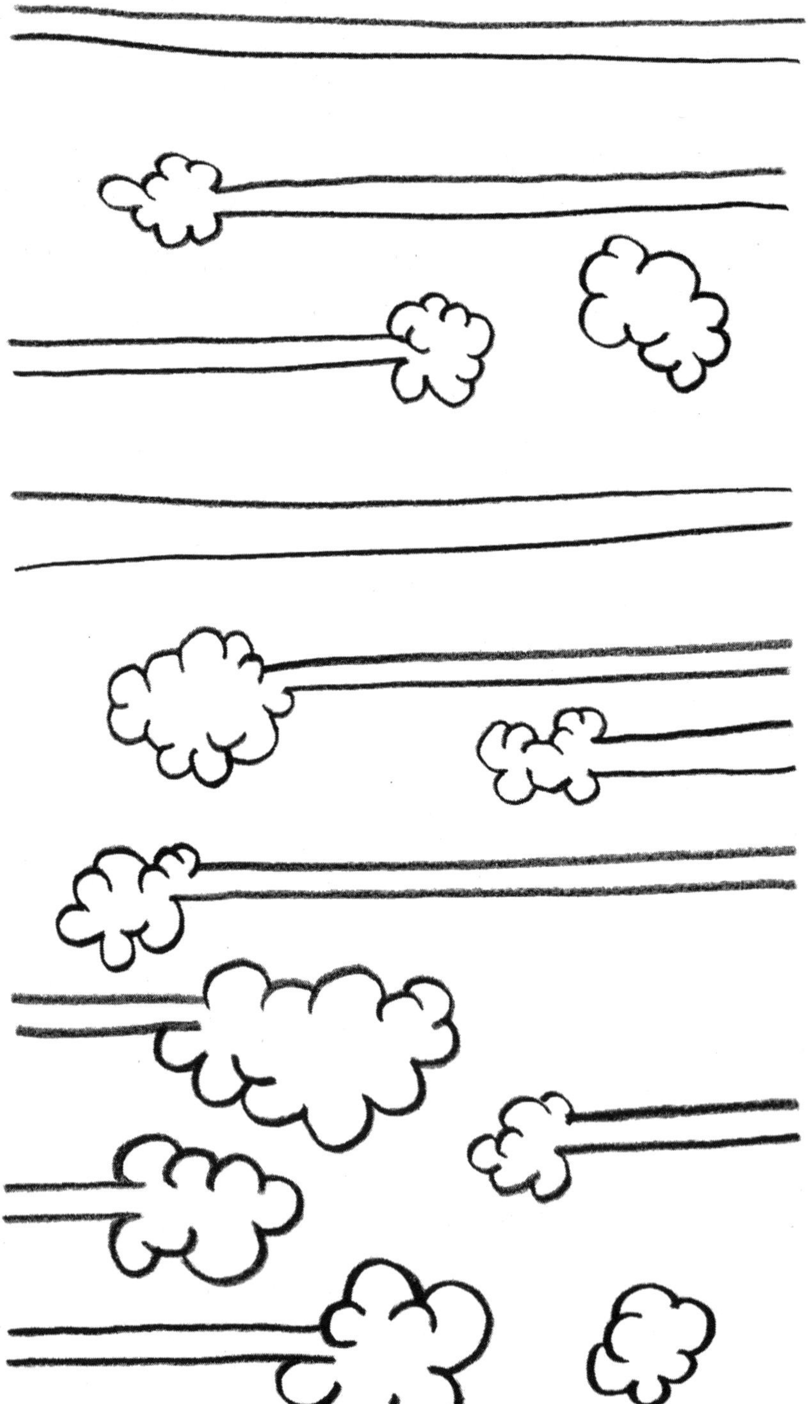

'HENRY KISSINGER is one of the world's highest-priced consultants, corporate directors, deal-makers and diplomatic fixers. When Henry Kissinger speaks, the world listens. And pays. The former U.S. Secretary of State has a lustre that has never worn off.' – The Montreal Gazette

POWER TALK

Whenever the sky
rains tears of blood
we see your faces
trying to hide
behind the clouds

Whenever bombs
or bullets flash
to silence the rumble from below
we see your fingers
caressing the buttons
and triggers

Whenever steel doors slam shut
on dissident voices
we hear your laughter
rattling the prison guard's keys

Whenever electric cattle prods
jab bare, quivering skin
to break a strike
or elicit a 'confession'
we trace the current
to a registered brainwave
from your sleep

Whenever people cry for
Justice and Dignity
you pop up
like brazen pimples
in your starched white shirts
your gold tie clips
holding back your rage

You never dirty your hands
you just remind your clients
behind closed doors
of the 'Free Market' prerogatives
tattooed on their skulls
And you urge them to act swiftly
turn back the hands of the clock
before it is too late

But remember:
whenever families gather crying
to bury their dead
we see your crooked smiles
etched so clearly
on the gravedigger's shovel
and we will not forget
we will never forget
because you haven't paid the real price
for your 'globalization' - yet

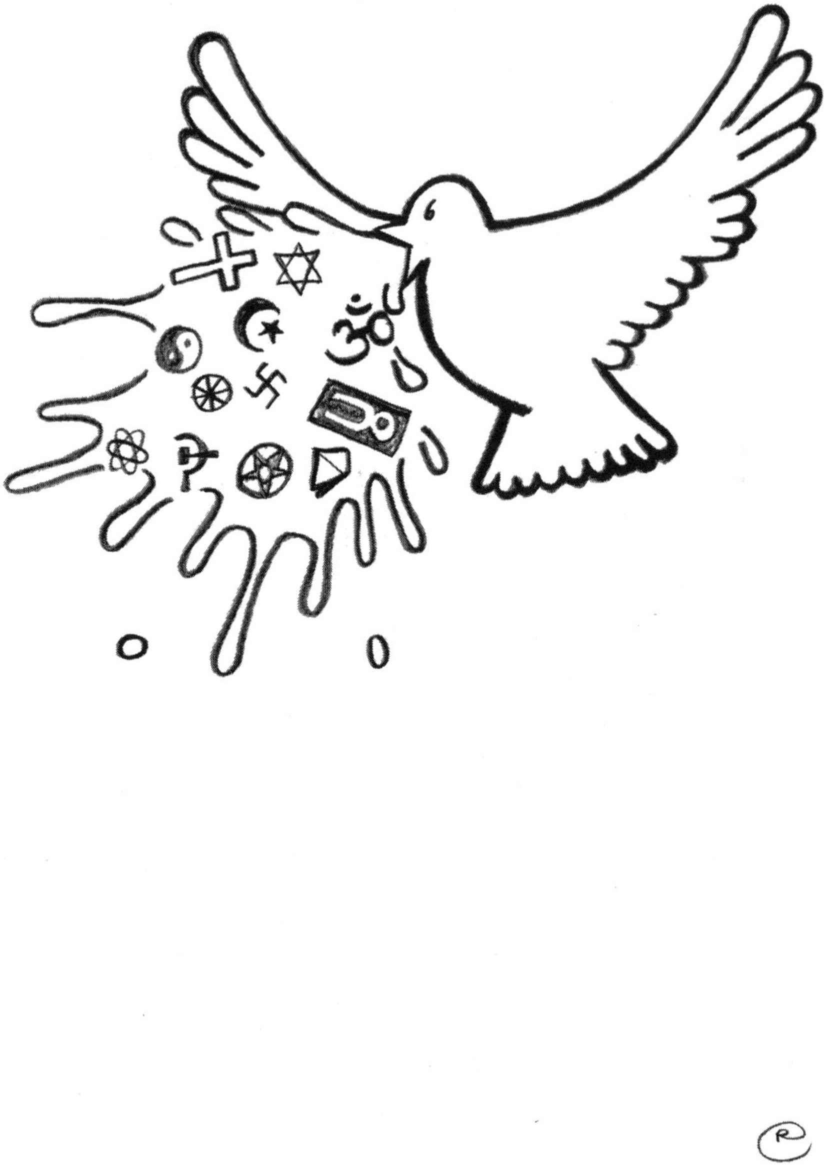

THE VELORUTION IS COMING!

The Velorution is coming!
Hear it spinning, spinning
No more cyclo-frustration
Free the planet! Free the people!
Bikesheviks revolting everywhere
Two-wheeled power, curb to curb
Wheel to wheel, clogging streets
forcing cars off the road with
Pedal Power! Pedal Power!
Cyclists of the world unite!
Free ourselves from the cars
Free the planet! Free the People!
Free us all from the tyranny
of Ford, GM, Honda and Jeep Cherokees
and gas guzzling mentalities
Crank it up! Roll the rubber!
Free ourselves from the dictatorship
of four-wheeled killers
from the death cult
of stinky Car Culture
Down with cars! Kill the cars!
Long live the Velorution of the Bike People!
All power to the Bikesheviks!
Cylce power everywhere!
Everyone cycling to overthrow the Car-tocracy!
Pedal Power! Pedal Power!
The Velorution is coming!
Hear it spinning, spinning
Jump on your bike – now!

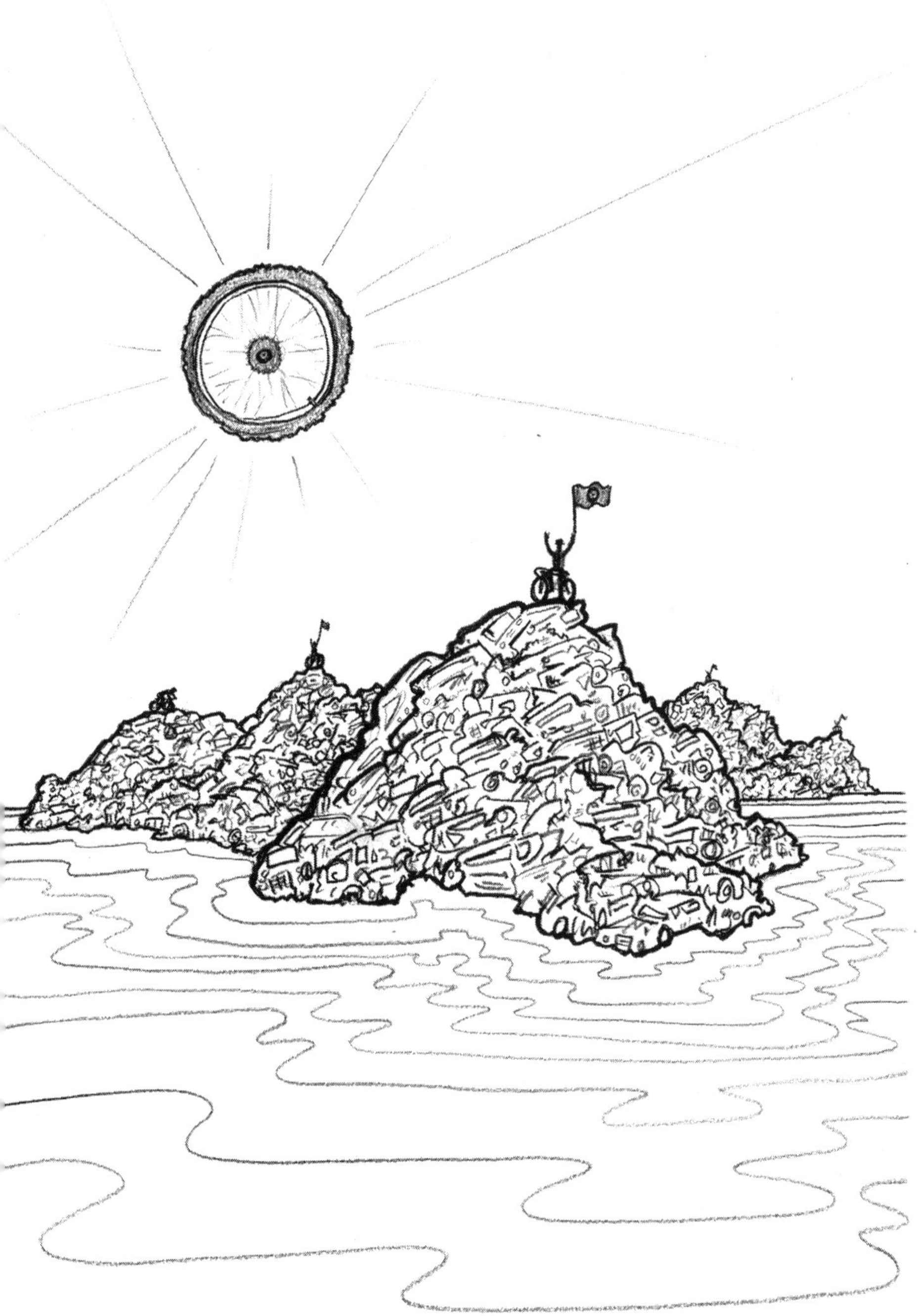

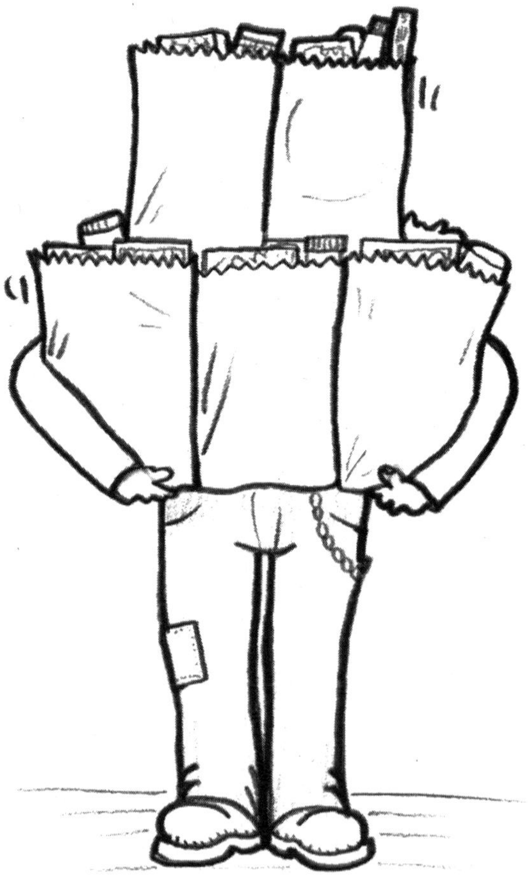

HOW TO SUPPORT A WORTHY CAUSE

Woke up brushed my teeth cut my thumb shaving burned the toast
then tripped on my kimono headfirst down the stairs to grab
the morning paper and Oops! Out falls a folded brown paper bag
embossed with a slimy local supermarket's dollar sign
and the exhortation in bold letters,
'YOU CAN MAKE THE DIFFERENCE'
'Whoopee!' I say and hobble back up the stairs to read how I,
a lonely citizen living in the shadow of the City
'can make the difference' to a scum-racked corporate food giant
that makes one hell of a difference to those who can't afford
to shop there but have little choice living far away from
alternative food stores.
Now they're telling me with their brown paper bag
gilded with corporate guilt to
'SUPPORT MONTREAL'S FOOD BANK'
and 'Help the underprivileged - give generously
by donating a few non-perishable food items to
SUPPORT A WORTHY CAUSE.'
Well hell! I'll support any worthy cause! I read the directions:
'Simply fill the provided paper bag with non-perishable food
products and deposit it in the barrel located at any of our
participating supermarkets.'
This corporate food giant has always been so charitable
to its shareholders fattening the leeches
while little old neighbourhood ladies scrounge nickels and dimes -
I see them at the checkout counter - to pay for dog food dinners -
but I never see them with dogs anywhere -
so how can I, a responsible citizen, refuse to
'SUPPORT A WORTHY CAUSE'?
I collect all my big brown empty paper bags
and head for my neighbourhood corporate supermarket
to show them exactly how I can

'MAKE THE DIFFERENCE' and 'SUPPORT A WORTHY CAUSE.'
I chain together a dozen shopping carts placing three empty
open bags in each one and push this clanking train of charity
down the aisles past the 'Perishables' and into the 'Land of
Non-perishables,' the canyons of cans and boxes and jars and zip
sealed tamper-proof packages and start to fill the bags chanting
'SUPPORT A WORTHY CAUSE, SUPPORT A WORTHY CAUSE!'
in time to the 48 squeaking wheels of my 12 rattling buggies.
I chuck in Chunky Canned Corn, Pacific Salmon, Giant Green Beans,
Polski Ogorki Pickles, Jumbo Cocktail Shrimp, the finest Coffee,
bags of Luscious Raisins, Crunchy Peanuts, Pineapple Rings,
Spicy Corned Beef, Imported Belgian Chocolate,
and Smoked Oysters from Korea, going easy on all the chemicals
and junk food, chanting my way up and down the aisles
like a Yogi out of the deep freeze:
'SUPPORT A WORTHY CAUSE, SUPPORT A WORTHY CAUSE!'
while other equally glassy-eyed, shopping numbed buggy pushers
around me – inspired by infectious good will and cosmic justice –
catch on and help toss in more non-perishables, chanting in unison
'SUPPORT A WORTHY CAUSE, SUPPORT A WORTHY CAUSE!'
Then quicker than a pot of boiling Uncle Ben's rice,
the 12 shopping carts were full and I was huffing and puffing
pushing and steering the charity train towards the Charity Barrel
on the other side of the cash registers when suddenly,
a Store Manager blocked my way with a
'What the hell are you doing?'
The Muzak didn't stop. The cashiers didn't bat an eye. The free
sample woman handing out thimblefuls of beer kept smiling.
Buggies empty and full went whizzing by while I,
proud with the rapturous look of a swelling heart replied,
I'M MAKING THE DIFFERENCE!'
as I pointed to the hundreds of other bright-eyed shoppers now
madly grabbing empty paper bags to fill themselves chanting

'SUPPORT A WORTHY CAUSE! SUPPORT A WORTHY CAUSE!'
The Store Manager was so touched he rolled his eyes heavenward,
to Head Office I thought, and fainted on the spot while I,
deciding at the last moment to by-pass the undersized Charity Barrel,
exited through the chrome gates, to Shopping Mall Central
Sitting Area where all the old timers, the regular glad-haners,
the retired and lonely locals hung out
I personally invited each to take a bag full of food,
because in the spirit of the times,
I was planning to return soon with hoards of neighbourhood
children to show them how easy it is to
'SUPPORT A WORTHY CAUSE'
with just an empty bag.

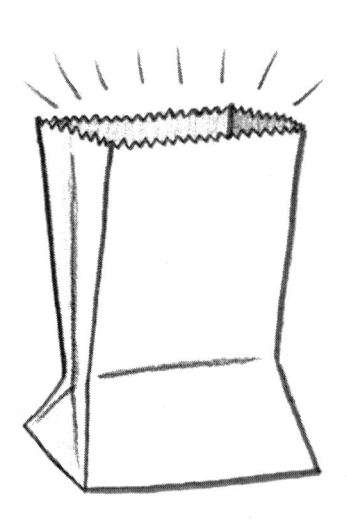

A WOBBLY DINNER

In St. Louis Missouri
one cold winter early in the 20th century
the city was full of the unemployed
They came from the wheat fields,
logging camps and mines
all freezing and starving tramping streets
without money or shelter
Among them were members
of the 'Industrial Workers of the World'
anarcho-syndicalists, 'Wobblies'
as they were known,
first class, shit-disturbing organizers
On cue, several hundred hungry men and women
invaded the city's restaurants
ordered the best meals, ate everything in sight
then, well-fed and smiling,
presented their bills to the managers
telling them to 'charge it to the Mayor'
Arrested, they gave passionate speeches in court
made front-page news
got people talking
Visions of thousands of the hungry unemployed
heading to St Louis to eat
at the Mayor's expense in or out of jail
spurred City Hall to pass an emergency bill
to provide housing, free beds and food
for those in need
Funny how a good meal
can make a difference

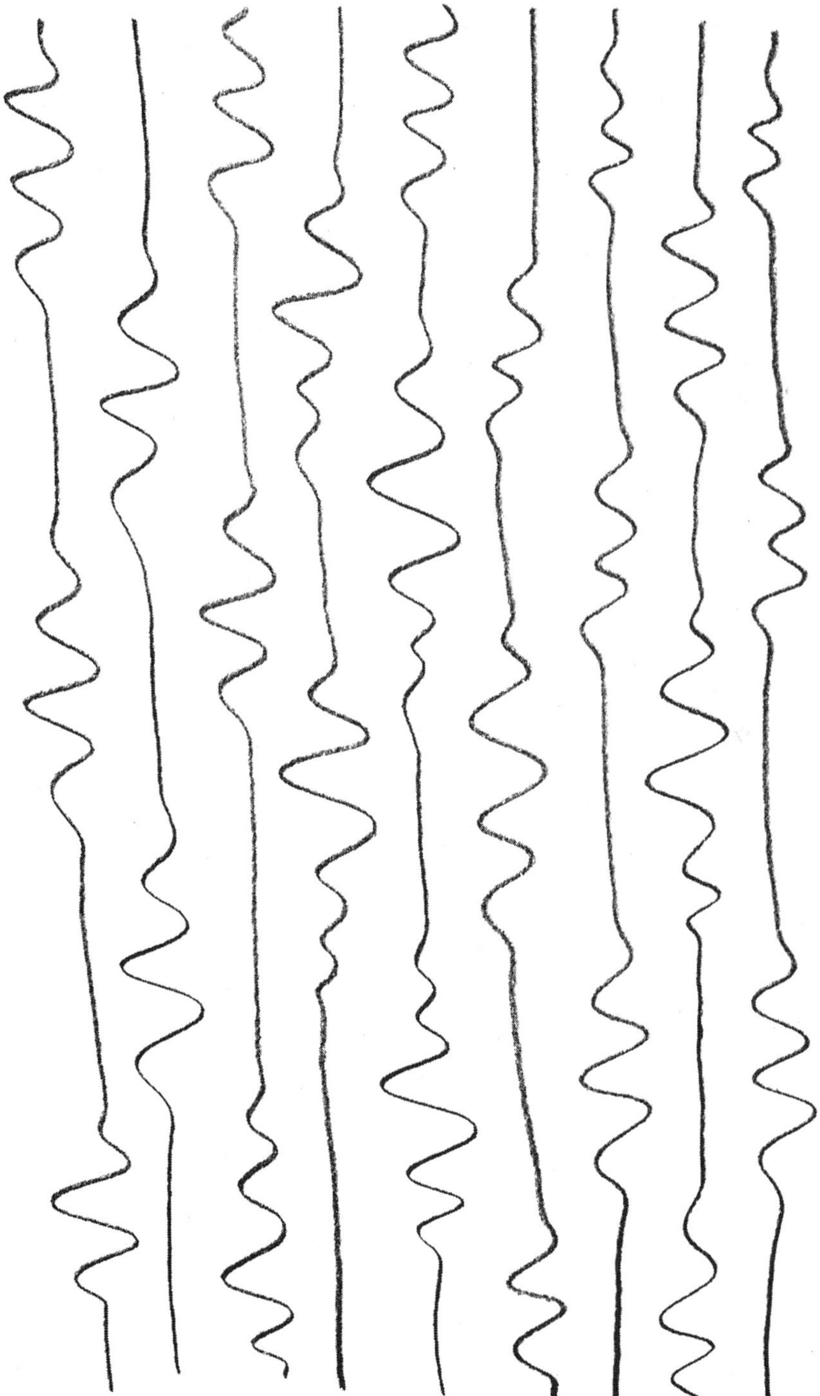

THE HACKER

I heard the RCMP recently picked up a 16-year old 'hacker'
who, in six months, penetrated a US army computer network
'At first I was like, excited,' he said.
'At the end it was, like lame, because it was so easy.
Like it was so sad. Our whole team, we hack to get better
and better stuff.'
Better and better stuff?

Hacker: I challenge you and your team
I challenge bored hackers everywhere:
HACKERS OF THE WORLD - LIKE UNITE!
In glorious cyber-guerilla revolution!

Hack into public transit scheduling
Put more buses and drivers onto the road
Hack into supermarket head offices
Drop the price of food
Hack into Welfare and Unemployment Insurance Offices
Increase everyone's cheques - threefold
Hack into government accounting departments
Show there really is more money for
daycares, hospitals, schools, social housing
Hack into news wire services and report a frenzied
all week giveaway of clothes and consumer goods
in all Wal-Marts (and if you're still bored)
Hack into the Pentagon, the Kremlin,
and disable their weapons
Hack into the CIA, the RCMP, CSIS
and secret police forces everywhere
Expose their dirty secrets to the world

Hack into every major corporate polluter
Hold them hostage until they agree to
invest in clean air, clean water, healthy food
and if they resist, shut 'em down
Hack into universities, lower their tuition fees
Hack into the Vatican, write pro-choice
and pro-contraception Papal decrees
Hack into the banks, erase all student loans
Deposit bank billions into the accounts of
poor people's groups and Zapatistas
Hack into Christian Fundamentalist sites
Flood them with images of happy, fucking couples
gay and straight

Hack into racist neo-nazi sites and replace them with pictures
of Barney using flame-throwers to neutralize nazis
Hack into McDonald's playpens and turn Ronald's smile
into a junk food frown as he throws up a billion burgers
Hack into the fortresses of the powerful and the greedy
Forbe's 500 richest men
bring them to their knees
demand that they hand over their fortunes or
you'll turn their Evil Empires into cyber-mush for dust mites
- then do it anyway
Hack away my friends, hack away!
It's the People's Cyber-Revolution, Cyber Pay Back Time
and you're the front line of cyber-guerillas!
So hack selectively, hack thoughtfully,
hack selflessly - but don't get caught!
Hack for Freedom! Hack for Justice! Hack for Anarchism!
Hack towards a better world for everyone
and we guarantee you won't be bored

MUTINY

Friends, are you worried sick
about your loved one fighting
some good-for-nothing war in a far off land?
    Well worry no more!
Send them a bottle of our revolutionary
new personal care product:
'MUTINY AFTERSHAVE' - the smell of rebellion!
With a little splash of MUTINY AFTERSHAVE,
your darling can save their sweet ass and come home alive.
Unlike other brands, MUTINY'S
    refreshing, secret formula
    interacts with the skin to help
    turn even the most timid
    submissive recruit into a
    bona fide, authority resisting rebel.

MUTINY AFTERSHAVE
    - lasting protection for the one you love!
The amazing powers of MUTINY AFTERSHAVE
were proven effective during the Viet Nam war.
In test after test, whole divisions of combat troops
refused to obey dangerous orders.
Entire companies sat down on the battlefield.
One whiff of this powerful, but subtle fragrance,
and unpopular officers and NCOs dropped dead.

Yes, there's something about a MUTINY man.
Each bottle of MUTINY AFTERSHAVE
comes with a handy foldout of how-to-do-it tips on desertion.
Makes fraternizing with the other side easy.
Doubles, too, as protection against sunstroke
and poisonous creatures of the night.
And don't forget - for her - we sell MUTINY SHAMPOO.
All the other women in her unit will say:

    'Gee your hair smells terrific!
    Let's put some sugar in the tank's gas tank!'

So go on friends. Do that soldier a favour.
Don't let them get wasted.
Get them a bottle of MUTINY AFTERSHAVE or SHAMPOO
and bring them back smelling good

GRANDMA'S REQUEST

Doreen's 82 year old grandma
who mothered 16 children
told her she had a dream:
'I dreamed about my 8 children
who died when they were small
They stood around my bed,
their chins propped up in their hands,
and they all said:
"Don't worry about us mama, we're all OK."
'My girl,' Doreen's grandma said,
'I want you to do me a favour.
Go to my children's graves in Batoche
tell them not to worry about me,
tell them I still love them and that I'm OK.'
And Doreen asked her grandma how
could she find the 8 graves and her grandma told her
'They each have a wooden cross, you'll see.'
So, under a blazing Prairie sun Doreen visited
the Métis cemetery high on a windswept bluff
overlooking a slow broad river
and found the wooden crosses –
a few hundred of them, each without a name
She couldn't be sure which were family, which not,
but she couldn't let her grandma down
So she visited each grave,
placed her hand on each wooden cross
and repeated softly, hundreds of times:
'If you are my grandma's child
you will know grandma sent me to tell you
she still loves you and you shouldn't worry about her
she's OK'

TIN CAN ALLEY

All the tin cans
rattlin' so loud
cats shudder past
hungry man prowls
Eyes the flowers
eyes the moon
spins on his heels, falls down
and moans:
'You spare my arms
You spare my legs
But you couldn't spare me
any food today'
Rolls his head
chews his tongue
spits out the blood
mourns the day
he was born:
'I need light
to defy the night
but you bury me
in your shadows
to keep me out of sight'
Bangs on a gate
his spit bloodies the world
he starts chewing his fingers
and mourns the betrayal
of the word:
'Who loves their brother?
Who gives, doesn't steal?
Who cherishes humanity?
Who'll give me a meal?'

Nothing left to chew
he rolls on the ground
stares up at the stars
mourns the lost and the found
wonders where are the stairs
once promised before:
'Wish upon a fat rat
Wish upon a toad
First sun in the morning
Feed me lumps of coal
A bit of gas light a match
lighten my load
Burn this shriveled body
Burn this skin and bones
Burn this hunger that's
driven me mad
The hunger you've
never known
Send the heavens
a soul that died homeless
condemned and alone
Then mark this spot your future:
another weed to grow

Chew the fingers down
Chew him to the ground
Chew the man people
stepped around

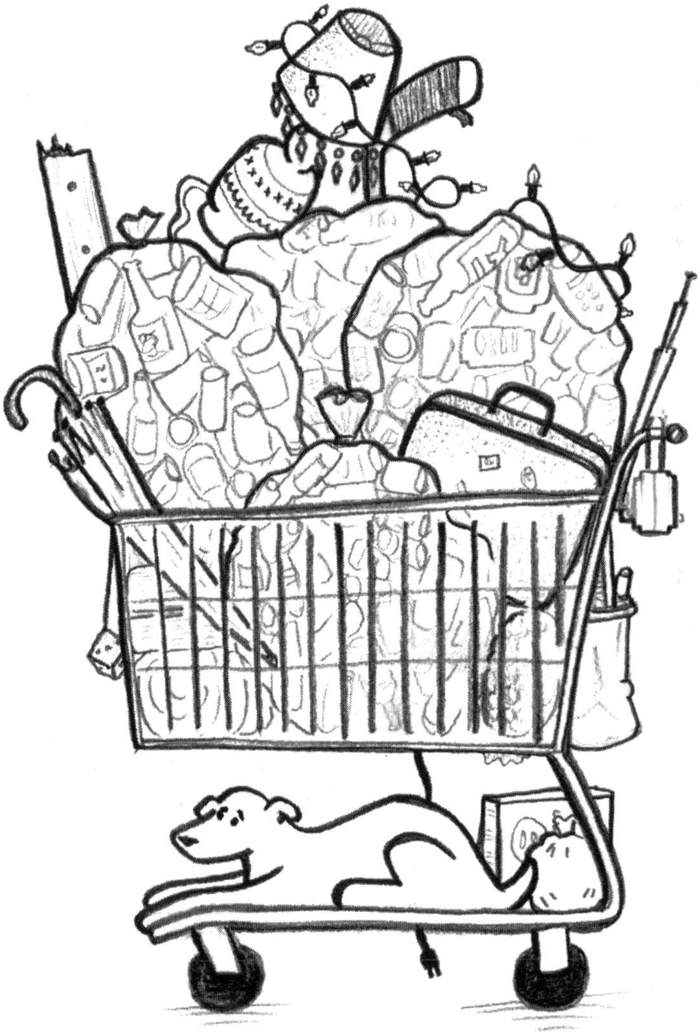

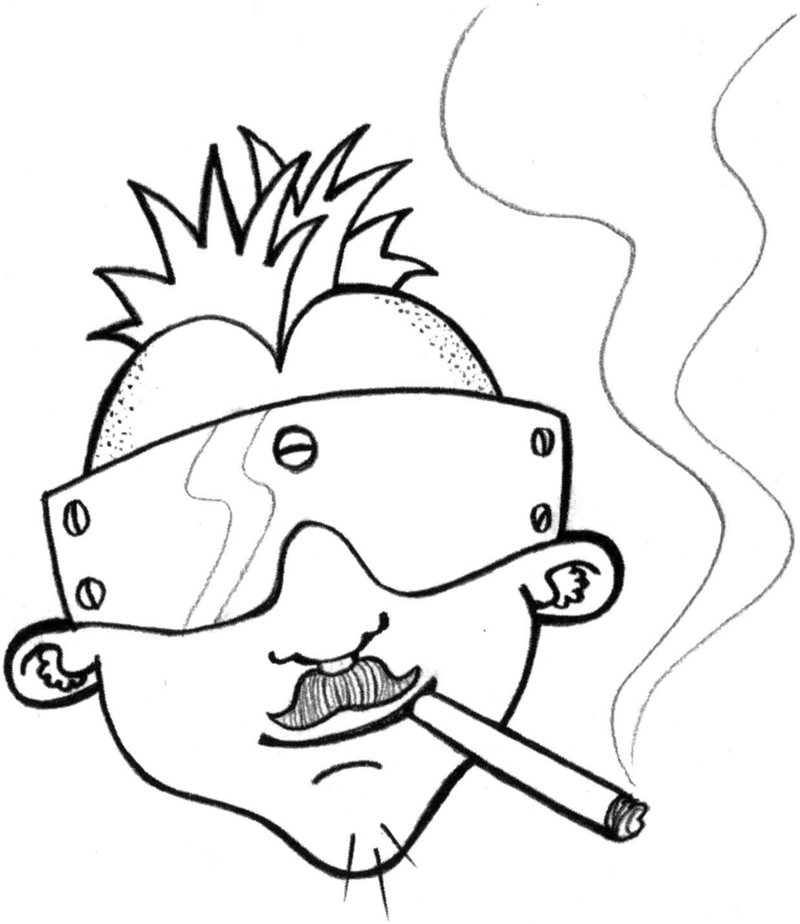

THINK REVOLUTION

Hey you Ms Girl Power Cool!
Hey you Mr Super-Cool Dude!
And you Hipster, Tripster, Dancer, Stoner, Raver
and you too, Mr and Ms Foreseeable
Future Unemployable!
Watcha gonna do
when they replace your burger-flippin'
barista serving guaranteed career choices
with cheaper and wholly automated dispensers
as in "Putcher monee in an' watchit spit out
da fries an' coffee" suckers?
It's a long way to Heaven
when you're riding the short road to Hell
just groovin' for the moment
trippin' on the music and the weed
nice and easy with the credit card
don't go too fast, make it last, but spend, spend, spend
smooth with the flow and the glow
of a city, a country, a fucking world in flames

So press 'Pause' – take a break from the party
and let's talk about Revolution Yee! Ha! OK?
Like not in Russia or China or Latin America
Not in Africa, Cuba, Florida or even on the TV
but right here in Canada, home of free beer – the concept
No, it's not another cheap marketing ploy
to cash in on a Che Guevera hot 'n spicy potato chip
nor a new better than cellular telephone Oh my God
technology you just have to have right now
but something much simpler

Press 'Rewind' and like, look around you:
Smell the air, take a deep breath without gagging
Feel the hot sun on your skin, time the burn
fastest one wins
Dare you to stick your foot in the harbour, lake or river
watch the totally cool rainbow-coloured guck gather round
Taste the newest genetically mutated tomato/potato, it bounces
Explain the *eau d'odeur* from your water tap
Ask yourself why your neighbours worry a lot -
it gives them wrinkles
Why old age pensioners eat dog food - it's gross
Why hospitals turn away the sick and the injured - it's unfair
Why some kids go to school hungry - really?
Why other kids sell their bodies and peddle drugs - cheaply
Why the richest among us don't give a shit - it's true!
Why those in power refuse to see
the garbage pickers swallowing ditched, leftover lunches
the kid prostitutes in the parks
the single moms slowly starving themselves
so their babies can eat
the rivers of quiet tears flowing out broken windows
and dingy, rat infested basement suites that suck
the disappearing birds, butterflies, marshes, lakes,
rain forests last seen near a black corporate hole
Like when's the last time you heard a frog croak
smelled fresh air or
weren't asked for spare change?

Remind yourself this isn't about Marx, or Lenin
or Communists or long forgotten way cooler Anarchists
or recent, lame revisionist historians
who tell us this is the end of history, the end of classes
that social dissent and mass, popular rebellion
are boring dated concepts
that Corporate Capitalism is here to stay
Hello? What solar system are they from?
This is about doing something
to radically change the way we live, OK?
to stop the rip-offs, the scams, the corporate crimes, OK?
'cause something is wrong, right?
Nothing is getting better,
it's getting worse, as in something funny is going on
So this is about Revolution
from below,
about you and me figuring out how we - together -
can stop the madness and like, take control -
of our own lives,
our own futures here and now
about us taking a break from the party
to talk about something different -
for a change

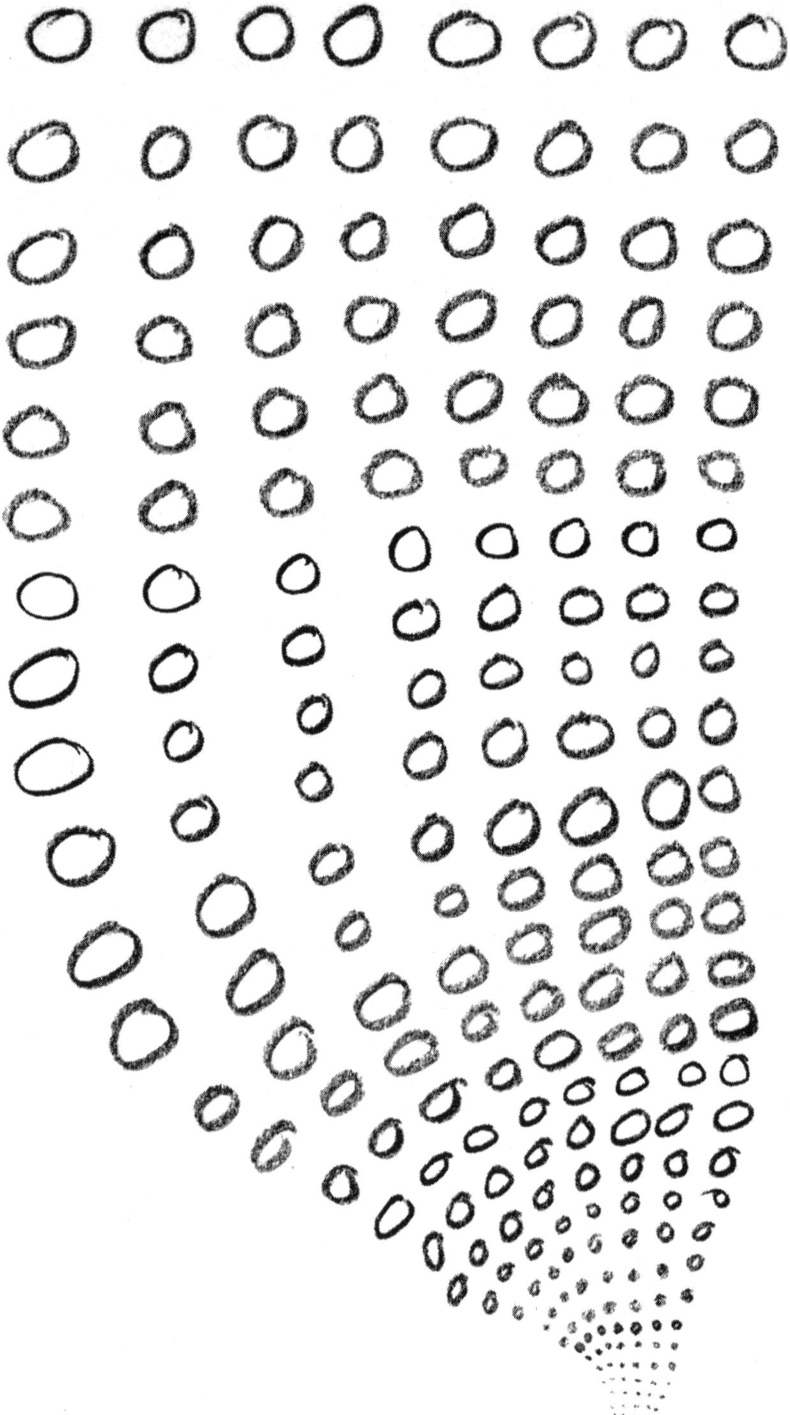

HETEROSEXUAL REINFORCEMENT PILL

Men: do you sometimes feel distanced from your wife,
girlfriend, or women in general?
Do you prefer to just hang out with the guys,
with no women present?

Do you find yourself unconsciously stroking, holding,
admiring hammers, baseball bats, beer bottles, pool cues,
and other phallic-like objects?

If so, these may be tell tale signs of potential latent
homosexual leanings, and you might need
a proven antidote right now:
HRP – the amazing Heterosexual Reinforcement Pills!

HRP's remarkable formula will help you fart, grunt and belch
your way back to heterosexual normalcy.
Guaranteed to cure all your symptoms and keep you straight.

Whether you live with a male roommate,
like the smell of aftershave,
or dream of guns and rocket launches,
you need HRP treatment now.
For fast and effective relief from those disturbing
'Oh my God, maybe I'm a homosexual!' panic attacks.
Helps stop that morning fear of waking up gay.
If you've ever had a momentary twang of doubt:

☐☐☐Heterosexual Reinforcement Pills.
☐☐☐For the uptight guy inside you.

DRY LOVE

I asked a woman friend
how she was doing
and she said, 'OK,'
except for her boyfriend troubles
in the bedroom
'My new boyfriend
doesn't know how to touch or please me
He refuses to go down on me
but always expects me
to give him a blow job
like it's my duty
Then he complains about my technique
He won't listen to me,
to what I like, to what turns me on
yet he can't understand
why I'm always dry
He says he's never had this problem before
He thinks he's such a fantastic lover
but I dread making love with him
He says it's my problem
and I should see a doctor'

My woman friend
is a doctor

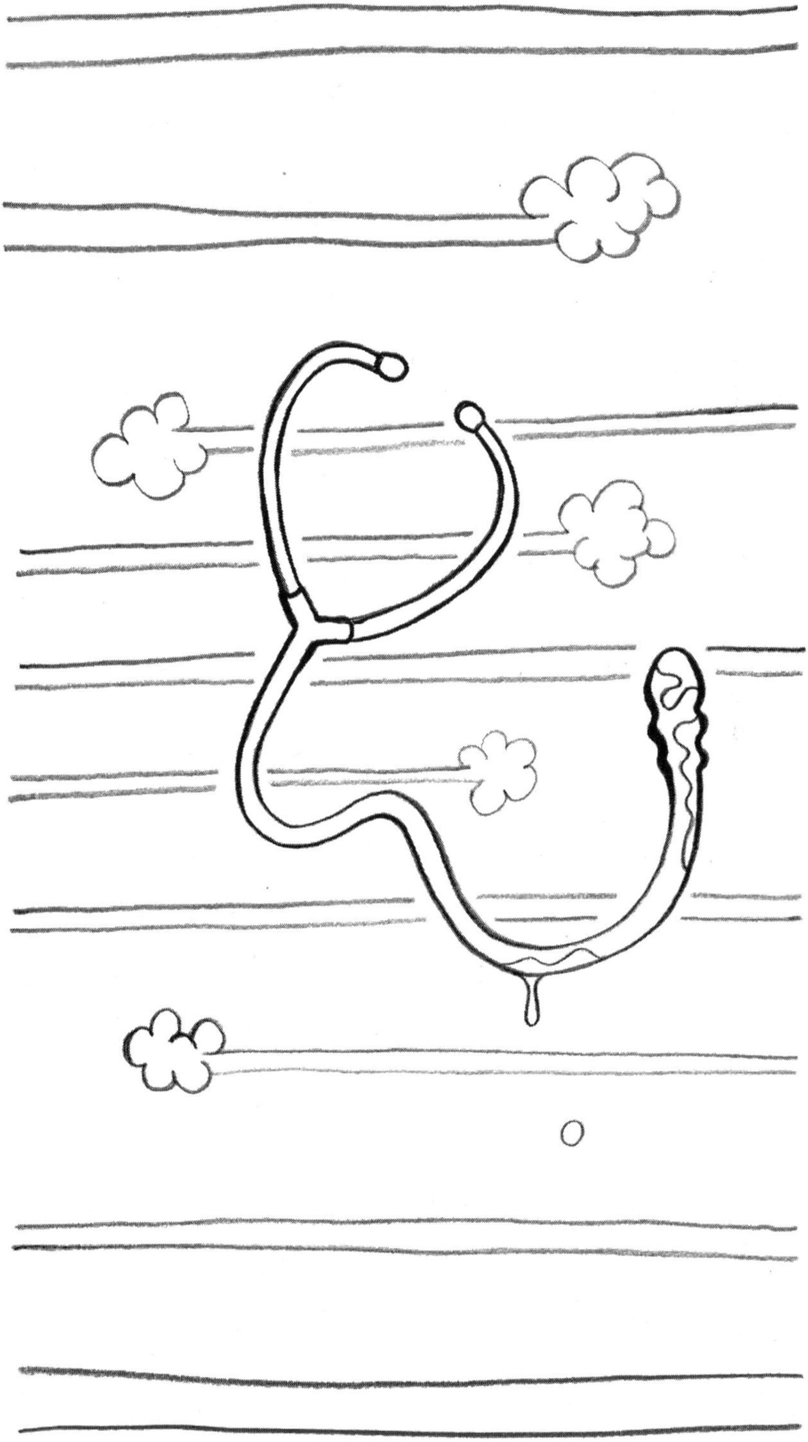

I WANT TO MAKE A CITIZEN'S ARREST

I want to arrest the Prime Minister of Canada
and charge his skinny little ass with violating
basic human rights
I want to arrest the Prime Minister of Canada
and charge him with gross criminal negligence
and crimes against the poor, women, children
the unemployed and underemployed, the sick and elderly
I want to charge him with contributing to
death and suffering from malnutrition, pollution,
inadequate health care, and growing impoverishment
He's the big boss
He calls the shots
He's cutting back social programs,
family subsidies, unemployment insurance, housing
programs, daycare subsidies, environmental watchdogs
He's living a great life
while Canadians slowly die

I want to arrest the Prime Minister of Canada
and charge him with lying,
distorting the truth and covering up
to serve his party and his faithful
It's 'his' fucking government, not ours
He never listens to us, only to paid lobbyists,
and those who surround him, stroke him,
and suck him off for favours

WANTED

I want to arrest the Prime Minister of Canada
and charge him, convict him and have him locked up
so he won't be a menace to Canadians any more
I want to see him behind bars, cleaning toilets and floors
because he terrorizes, robs and poisons Canadians
He is a wanted man
and I want him removed from office – now
And to save taxpayers money
I also want to arrest all his henchmen:
his ministers, upper level bureaucrats,
his yes men and women
One mass civil arrest in the name of humanity
It can't be that complicated
We have millions
of witnesses to testify against them
Once they're all locked up
we'll save billions in salaries,
payoffs, kickbacks, travel allowances, armored
limos, planes and bathrooms
to reinvest for the good of the people
Of course we'll empty the prisons
of all the innocent and the poor
to make room for the politicians,
but they shouldn't complain about
bunking with neo-Nazis, KKK
and the Aryan Brotherhood
They have friends in common
They're in the same line of work
and deserve the same reward:
Life with each other

TEARS ARE TRUE

I saw a grown man cryin'
sittin' on the stairs
I said
'Watcha doin' cryin'
sittin' on the stairs?'

He said
'The Truth's gone and left me
sittin' on the stairs
I'm all alone now
sittin' on these stairs'

I said
'If the Truth's gone and left you
sittin' on these stairs
Get up and we'll go find it
somewhere else'

'It's probably round the corner'
I said, 'Come walk with me
It's probably round the corner
Come on, you'll see
Let's go find it,
Come walk with me'

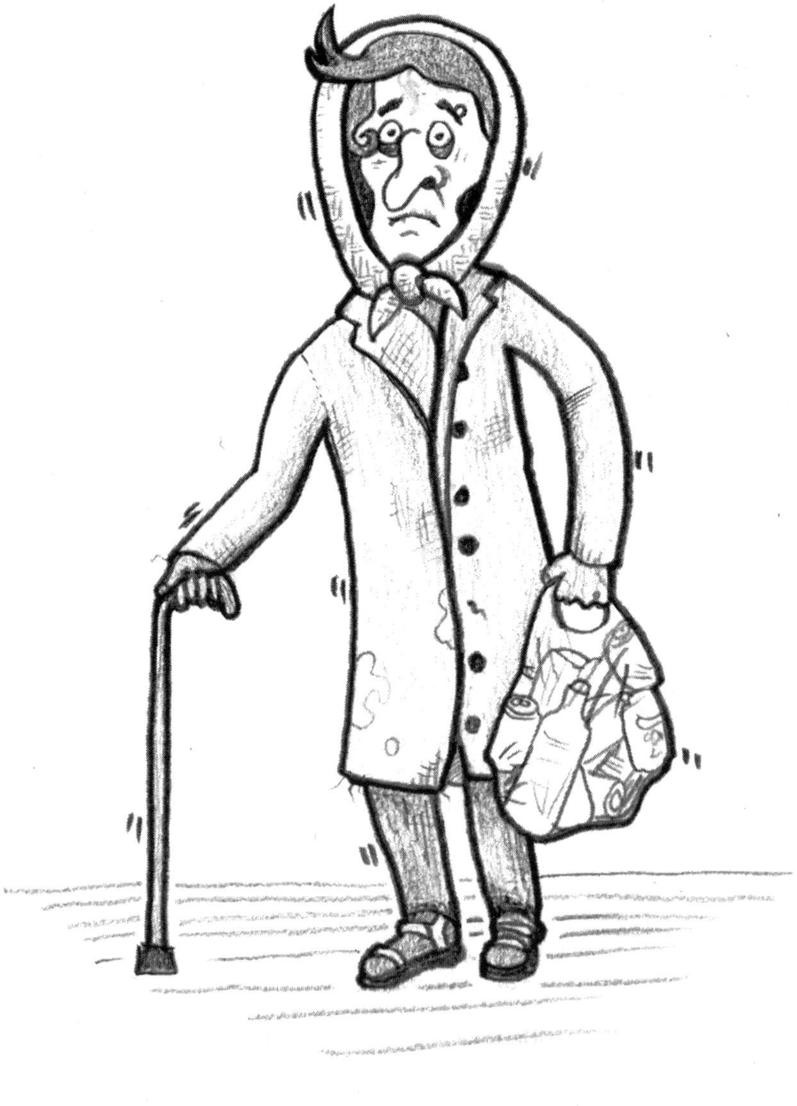

SHE WALKS WITH A CANE

She walks with a cane
tap tapping the sidewalk
arthritic legs
Babushka on head
Dusty sandals stockinged feet
Her face reads
East meets West and old age
Hand rummages in the garbage can
Food or bottles, food or cans
This country so good to her
whizzes by
in rush hour foot traffic
She's caught in the stream
of youth and jungle beats
platform shoes and
swish swish pants jackets and tongues
hiding something
from the gaze of old women like her
She tries to catch eyes and ears
to tell them
it's too much / it's not enough
it's here / it's so far away
it's ready / it won't stop
it's time
time to say something

MONTRÉAL

MONTREAL, YOU'VE GOT NOT HEART, NO ART

Montréal!
You've got no heart, no art
only bars pumping beer into the veins
of the vain on the Main
contemplating the pain of heartless,
artless pleasures on sale in
les boutiques sales, les boutiques
qui vendent ce qui est chic
the chic stamped 'Void,' 'No Trespassing,'
'Trendy terrorism' to terrorize the trend less
who've tasted fate and found it tasteless
who've mortgaged their soul to a BMW,
a belching, motorized wart

Montréal!
You've got no heart, no art
in your shiny towers spitting out dead air
that's conditioned to preserve the hair
under your conservative chin
And in your bleached hair, your dessert lairs
your tacky fairs where all the laughter
is imported, professional, repackaged and
sold to the bored who otherwise question
their own sense of humour
because in this City of Celebration
the drinks are never on the house, eh?
Dare we ask:
Is the beer overpriced only for those who can afford it?
Can you lend me what you spend at the end of your day?
Can you refill my paper cup with pieces of crust,
the end butts and spare change your Yuppies
guard under their pillows?
Can you smile on me the toothless smile
of a bent longshoreman who no longer knows
where all the ordinary guy's taverns have gone
tabarnac, or if it's just his imagination
that's harboured a thirst too long?

MON✝REAL

Montréal!
You've got no heart, no art
only barbecued *vedettes*
this year's warmed up star
to serve the hungry already tired
of feeding on themselves
But watch it:
You've tried hard, and can't consume me
I'm inedible, dirty, and I reek of garlic
and raw green onions
I walk you, talk to you,
caress your sidewalks with my ragged soul
I scream your name when I sit on the toilet
and the pleasure is all mine

Montréal!
I came here looking for love, for dignity
and all I found was asbestos, mercury, two stones
a cross, and a mountain begging for mercy

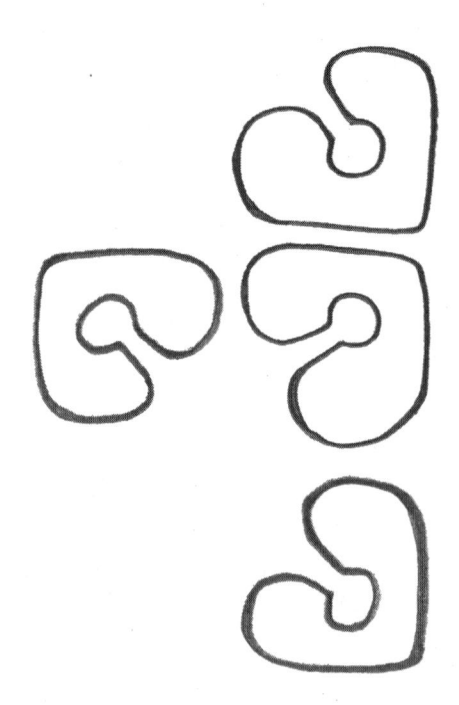

Montréal,
You don't forgive the French
You don't forgive immigrants
You don't forgive your poor
If they drink your water
they reel and totter
Instead, you hand out tickets:
one for free films
for free concerts
free frits with each doughnut that
comes through the door
so we eat you, Montréal,
your rats, mice, pigeons,
curb by curb,
burping, choking, farting our way
from corner to corner hoping the
dépanneur will cash in your partygoer's
empties – how they weigh us down

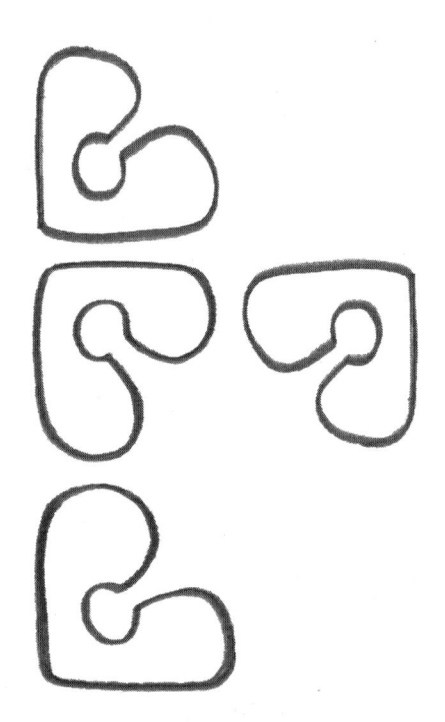

Montréal!
You got no heart, no art
Your mailboxes don't go 'BOOM!'
anymore in the middle of the night
Your streets aren't rocked by exploding *fleurs-de-lys*
Your soldiers sleep the peace of the silent
truce each rebel has made with your clothing stores
You send in the riot squad, the SWAT team,
the Army to make medical history on your own gut
while you lay naked, shameless,
exposed in all your glory to drooling investors,
the microchip dealers in final art
who nod their approval then grab
and squeeze you by the balls
Montréal, Stop the Metro!
I want to get off!
I want to warn
the jumpers ahead
it ain't worth it
don't die for this!
I want all the passengers to get off
and trade places for a week and write letters
to *La Presse, The Gazette* about you,
about all of us stuck on this island
shipwrecked in the middle of an unread river

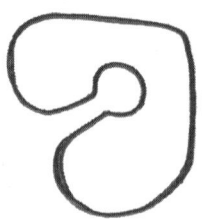

Montréal!
It's St Jean-Baptiste Day and the Baptistes want your head
All good Christians burn your churches to the ground
Your Ritz was never ritzier, your hungry so thin,
the lines for a handout, please, so long
Sure, you can pretend to celebrate Life,
Profit and Boom Boom Times to come of
a once official Boom Pa Pa Party town
But who sleeps in your broken buses
stacked alongside your tracks?
Who calls the side of the Mountain
under a lone spruce, 'home'?
Who carved their initials into your streets
with the bullets from a Mohawk machine gun?
Pierre? Josephine? The 'Oh Canada' man?
A Chinese cook from NDG? A bagel boy from
El Salvador who couldn't stand the heat?

Montréal!
how many more caribou will die
to light up Place Ville Marie?
To open and close
the Olympic Stadium roof?
To power toothbrushes in Manhattan?

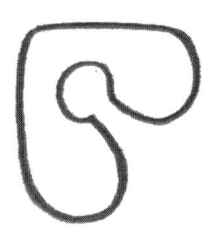

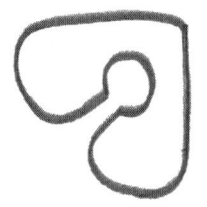

Montréal, face it
You got no heart, no art
yet you flaunt your manicure like a
blue-rinse from Hampstead:
"Look Toronto, same colour bricks"
"An we speak Eng-leash"
Go on,
Sweep the streets clean of undesirables,
hide to poor somewhere behind an empty gas
station in the suburbs
Let the bourgeois reclaim the inner city
because they pay for the police helicopters
that make them feel safe at night
Do whatever you can to silence the growing cancer
because the healthy still dine on sidewalk terraces
20 feet from snarling traffic
Toast your masters from the past,
because Montréal,
today no one can afford your masters
living, dead, nailed to a wall or hung from
the nearest rusty lamppost
Montréal, I hear your cracked trumpets
wherever I go, and I travel far,
but nowhere in this city of thin walls is far enough

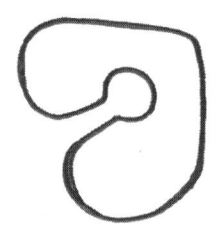

MONTREAL

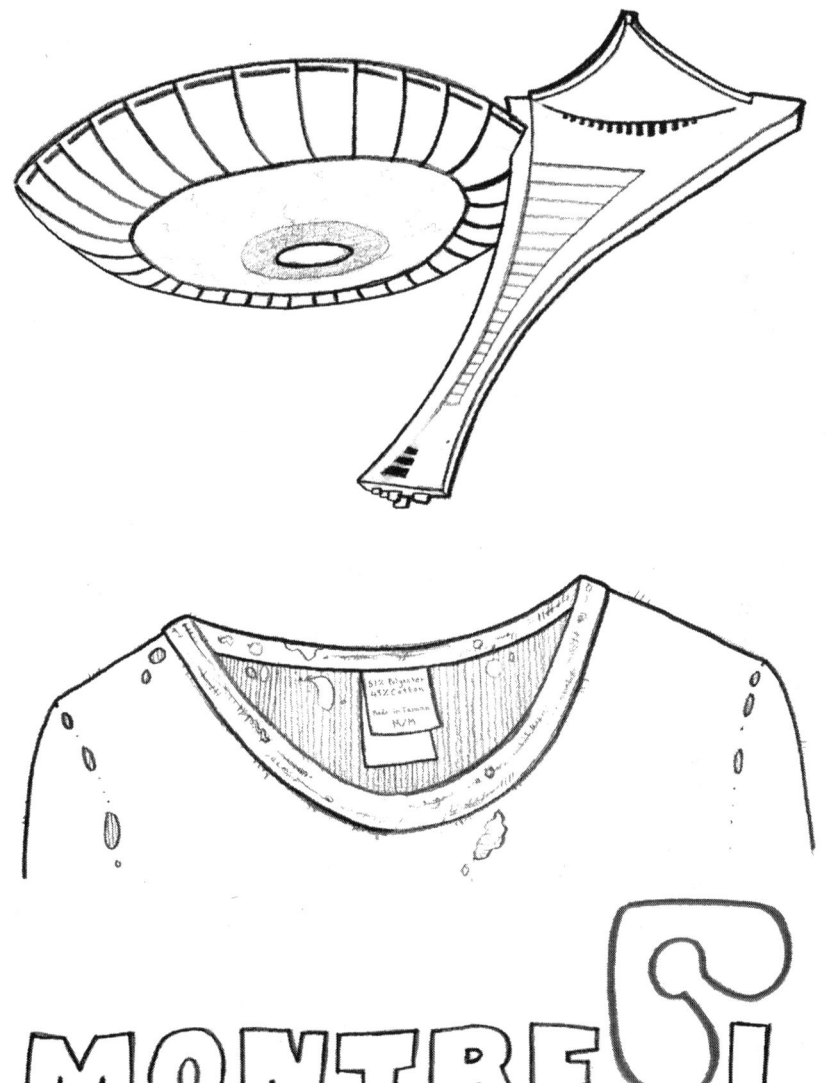

"*Encore!*" echos *Places des Arts* as an opera
company truck snuffs out Charlie who was asleep
under some cardboard up against a hot air grill
"Bravo!" goes Radio Canada as Mrs D lovingly
washes another ruby red tomato plucked from
the Pine Ave garden no one warned her
was hazardous to her health
Bravo Montréal!
'Cause you got no heart, no art and the world knows
Your children sing along to MTV
while their teeth drop out keys of B flat, F sharp,
the yellowed seeds no one will plant to guarantee your future
Your dogs keep marking their territory
in front of condos marked *'vendu'*
Montréal!
Who bought you so cheap and swept you
onto the market when the janitor wasn't looking?
Will an American trade you for a winning team?
Will you wither away during the next beer strike?

Montréal!
You got not heart, no art
only the hangers on
Evictees from St Norbert, St Hubert, St Denis streets
and all the Saints who failed them in their demands
for tenants' rights, tenants' grace, tenants' revenge
forgotten families splattered on your sidewalks,
street-walkers pushed up and robbed against your walls
welfare babies crammed into your basements
the garbage pickers thwarted by your locks
You mail jackpot pot keys to everyone on my block
and expect us to turn them in when we gas up?

Montréal,
I'm running on empty through
your darkened streets
with a brick in my hand
Your window is big, new, tinted green to match the
last tree on my block
The sign in it says "Vente, on sale, special"
I sniff the flowers
raise my head
see the mountain cross in flames now
brighter than any festival of fireworks
and with all my strength
I hurl the brick
without letting go
Montréal!
You've got no heart, no art
but tons of bricks waiting

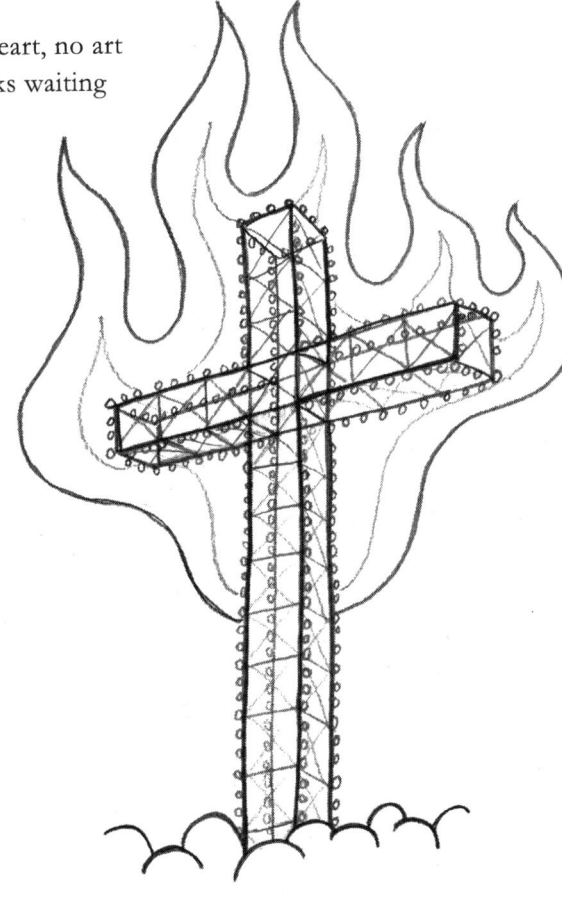

DISCOGRAPHY NORMAN NAWROCKI

Solo & with his different bands
CROCODILE LIVE A QUEBEC CITY - cass, 2014, Croco Records, Montreal
CAZZAROLA! - CD, 2013, Les Pages Noires, Montréal
LETTERS FROM POLAND / LETTRES DE POLOGNE - CD, 2006, LPN, Mtl
SANN - CD, 2005, LPN, Mtl.
DUCK WORK - CD, 2004, LPN, Mtl.
THE MONTREAL MANHATTAN PROJECT - CD, 2004, LPN, Mtl.
DAZOQUE! - CD, 2002, LPN, Mtl.
FIGHT TO WIN! - CD, 2001,
G7 Welcoming Committee Records, Winnipeg
I DON'T UNDERSTAND WOMEN! - cass, 1993, LPN, Mtl.
OVERDALE RAG - cass, 1987, Jelly Bean, Montreal, Mtl.

With Rhythm Activism
JESUS WAS GAY - CD, 1998,
G7 Welcoming Committee Records, Winnipeg
BUFFALO, BURGERS & BEER - cass, 1995, LPN, Mtl.
MORE KICK! - CD, 1995, LPN, Mtl. / Konkurrel, Amsterdam
BLOOD & MUD - CD, 1994, LPN, Mtl. / Konkurrel, Amsterdam /
Cass, 1997, Nikt Nic Nie Wie, Warsaw, Poland
TUMBLEWEED - cass, 1993, LPN, Mtl.
OKA II - cass, 1992, LPN, Mtl.
WAR IS THE HEALTH OF THE STATE - cass, 1991, LPN, Mtl.
OKA - cass, 1990, LPN, Mtl.
PEROGIES, PASTA & LIBERTY - cass, 1990, LPN, Mtl.
FIGHT THE HIKE! - cass, 1990, LPN, Mtl.
UN LOGEMENT POUR UNE CHANSON - cass, 1990, LPN, Mtl.
LOUIS RIEL IN CHINA - cass, 1988, LPN, Mtl.
RESIST MUCH - OBEY LITTLE - cass, 1987, LPN, Mtl.
RHYTHM ACTIVISM "LIVE" - cass,1987, LPN, Mtl.
RHYTHM ACTIVISM - cass, 1986, LPN, Mtl.

Compilations (solo & with all his bands)
DUETS FOR ABDELRAZIK - CD, 2012, Howl! Arts Collective, Montreal
ART, ANARCHY AND ACTIVISM - CD, 2007, CBC Radio, Toronto
TAKE PENACILIN NOW- CD, 2005,
G7 Welcoming Committee Records, Winnipeg
SPOKEN BROKEN - CD, 2004, Wired on Words, Mtl.
2 TONGUE 5 - CD, 2004, Loose Discs, Quebec
ANARCHIST BLACK CROSS - CD, 2003,
ABC Records, Sao Paolo Brazil
LOVE & RAGE VOL 1 - CD, 2003, Love & Rage Records, North Richmond, Australia
2 TONGUE 4 - CD, 2003, Loose Discs, Quebec
BEYOND 'MAN' HOOD, cass, 2001, Montreal Men Against Sexism Prod, Montréal
RETURN OF THE READ MENACE - CD, 1999, G7 Welcoming Committee Records, Winnipeg
PASAZEER - CD, 1999, Pasazer Records, Warsaw, Poland
FOLKOPHOBIA - CD, 1998, Tranzophobia, Chambery, France
LES MYSTERES DES VOIX VULGAIRES #3 - cass, 1997, Art as Hammer Records, Milano, Italy
LES MYSTERES DES VOIX VULGAIRES #2- CD, 1997, Art as Hammer Records, Milano, Italy
LESS ROCK MORE TALK - CD, 1997, AK Press, San Francisco/Edinburgh
KESKIDEEZ - EP, 1997, Broken Ear, California
UP TO D.A.T. - CD, 1997, Mad's Collectif, Saint-Etienne, France

KING KONK 2 - CD, 1996, Konkurrel, Amsterdam
ZOOCOMPILATION - CD,/cass, 1996, Trottel Records, Budapest, Hungary
UNIRACIAL SUBVERSION - CD, 1995, Blackbird Records, Hong Kong
CRISES - CD, 1994, Broken Tapes, Limesay, France
MAIS OU EST PASSE L'ANARCHIE? - cass, 1994, Broken Tapes, Limesay, France
POGO AVEC LES LOUPS - CD, 1992, On a Faim!, Paris
BITTERSWEET CANADA - CD,/cass, 1992, Word of Mouth Records, Toronto
ZWOLNA TAPES VOL 1 - cass, 1992, Zwolna T & R, Metz, France
NIGHTMARE ON ALBION STREET - LP, 1992, 1 in 12 Records, Bradford, England
BRAIN BATTERY - cass, 1991, Broken Tapes, Limesay, France
JUST LISTEN - cass, 1991, All Genre, Waltham, MA
LES MYSTERES DES VOIX VULGAIRES - CD, LP, cass, 1990, Divergo, Milano, Italy
SUR LA GUERRE DES SEXES (ABOUT SEX WAR) - LP, 1990, P.A.I., Paris
THEFT OF PARADISE - cass, 1988, Technawabe Sounds, Ottawa
CIA TAPES - cass, 1988, Blurg Records, Bradford, UK
VOICE OF AMERICANISM - cass, 1988, Bad Newz, New York
EXPO HURTS EVERYONE - 7", 1986, Sudden Death Records, Vancouver

PHILTRE BIOGRAPHY

'Philtre' is the pen name of the Montreal artist Philippe Caron. He collaborated with Norman Nawrocki on the design and production of this new edition of **No Masters! No Gods! Dare to dream** and created original illustrations cover-to-cover exclusively for the book.

Born in Trois-Rivières in 1979, Caron has been working in diverse Montreal arts scenes for over fifteen years. Graphic design, illustration, painting, music, education sciences – the spectrum of his interests is as broad as his imagination. He appreciates all kinds of beauty expressed in its purest form or in the most eclectic manner. A lover of contrasts of all kinds, he does not hesitate to resort to provocation to bring art to life in the miracles of daily existence.

Caron's paintings which intrigue through their simplicity and truthfulness have been featured in several galleries:
Philippe Caron Autiste peintre, Patro Vys, Montreal, 2006
Philtre as a Freak Release, Our Studio, Berlin, 2006
O Kanata, Histoire d'hier pour les yeux d'aujourd'hui,
Galerie Zone Orange inc., Montreal, 2007
Philippe Caron, Art en vue, UQAM, Montreal, 2007
9408 petits carons, Le boudoir, Montreal, 2010

He also plays electric and acoustic bass in local bands: Brain Püker (1993-1996), Double Snare (2001-2004), Crazydent (2005-2008), Drama Culture (2009-2014) and Crocodile (2013-).

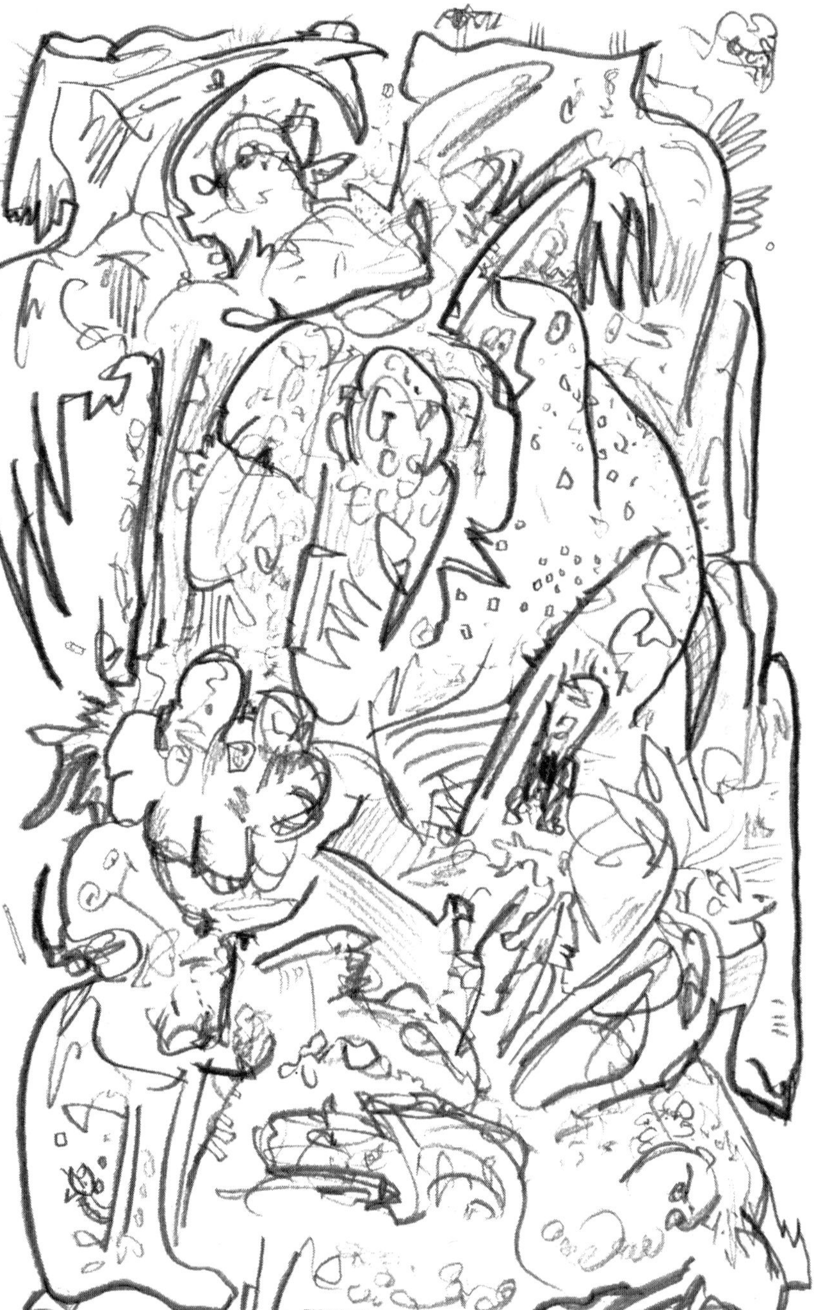

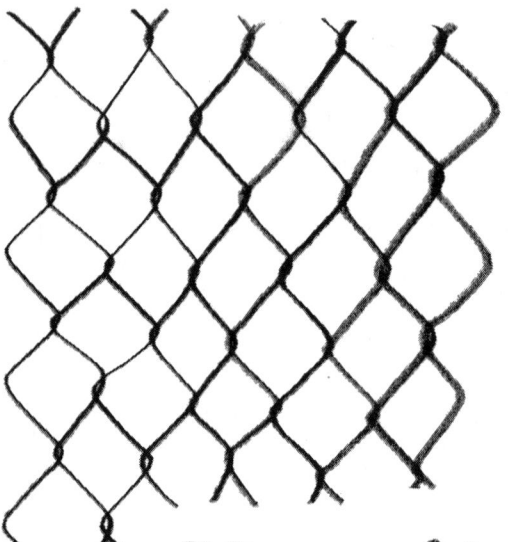

Vous êtes ici.

You are here.

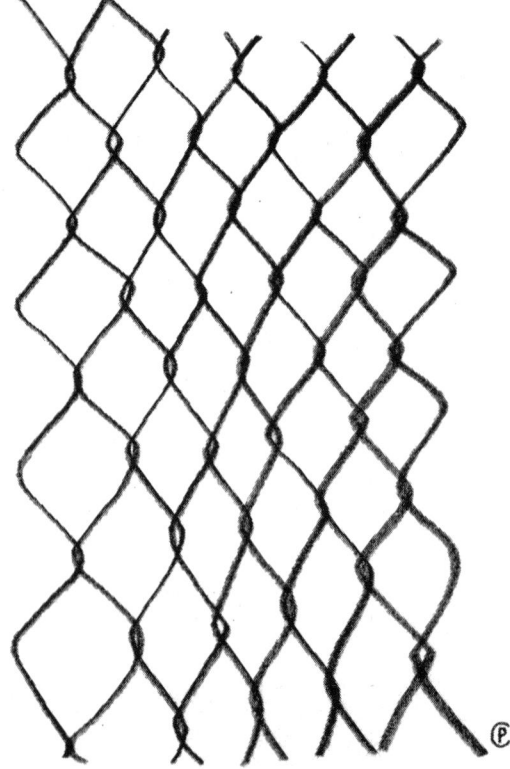

LES PAGES NOIRES (LPN) is a non-profit, volunteer-run, multi-media publishing, recording, production and distribution project based in Montreal, Quebec, Canada. The project is dedicated to helping create and disseminate dissident, freedom-loving, anarchist-inspired culture that promotes social justice.

FRIENDS OF LPN: LPN operates on the margins with obvious financial constraints that limit the number and frequency of our artistic creations. We welcome outside financial contributions from those who want to support our work. If you'd like to help us: rhythm@nothingness.org

MORE FROM LES PAGES NOIRES DISTRIBUTION, MONTREAL

BOOKS

Déjeuner pour anarchistes, poésie by Norman Nawrocki, 104 pages, illustrated. The French translation of Nawrocki's classic 'Breakfast for Anarchists.'

RED: Quebec Student Strike and Social Revolt Poems by Norman Nawrocki, 104 pages. Beautifully bound and illustrated book of his poems documenting the largest ever civil disobedience movement in Canadian history: the 2012 Quebec post-secondary 'red square' student strike.
'(Nawrocki is) a Montreal legend.' – The Gazette, Montreal

The Anarchist & The Devil do Cabaret by Norman Nawrocki, 207 pages. Internationally lauded collection of his short stories, letters and journal entries inspired by a Rhythm Activism band tour of Europe.
'Mirrors the best of cabaret, blending artistry, comedy, and protest into an anthem for social justice.' – Amazon.ca

BOOKS

Breakfast for Anarchists by Norman Nawrocki, 80 pages, illustrated. The first volume in Norman Nawrocki's Brain Food Trilogy. Over 30 provocative, poetic capsules of Nawrocki's trademark wit, passionate rage, love and reflection. Includes his celebrated piece, *Why am I an anarchist?*

Lunch for Insurgents by Norman Nawrocki, 80 illustrated. More radical poems songs and rants about how thinking imaginative citizens can engage in simple everyday creative resistance.
'One of Canada's most active activist scribes'
– The Vancouver Province

Dinner for Dissidents by Norman Nawrocki, 80 illustrated. A powerful, rabble-rousing dose of poetic creativity for anyone craving new ways of thinking towards a world without rulers or ruled. Soul-stirring poems, songs and lyrical musings.

Nightcap for Nihilists by Norman Nawrocki, 80 illustrated. Continues Nawrocki's obsession with hammering away poetically at a rotting social order and replacing it with a newly liberated, more just world. Both a battle-cry and an anarchist vision of what's wrong and what to do.

MUSIC

CAZZAROLA! (CD) by Norman Nawrocki & amici (friends). The musical soundtrack for his novel Cazzarola! Anarchy, Romani, Love, Italy (PM Press, 2013). www.cazzarola.ca.
Sixteen tracks of original and traditional Italian-themed songs (from 1880 today) composed & recorded by Nawrocki and the bands Crocodile, DaZoque!, DisCanto, E Zhivindi & more, in Italy & Canada. Music inspired by or related to his novel.
'A blend of Italian folk, sprinkled with a little world beat, which serves as a haunting yet still soothing soundtrack for his novel of the same name' – The Gazette, Montreal

Letters from Poland / Lettres de Pologne (CD) by Norman Nawrocki Nawrocki plays looped violin, viola, accordion, piano and a 142-string Ukrainian/Polish tsymbaly (hammered dulcimer) and reads 12 letters from The Anarchist & The Devil Do Cabaret sent to his father from a Polish uncle. Poignant, humourous and bittersweet, the letters trace the love and longing of one brother for another and document his growing resistance to Nazism.

Duck Work (CD) by Norman Nawrocki
A beat-rich, anti-war, anti-Empire onslaught of hypnotic bass, percussive and driving looped violins, viola and cello, with incendiary lyrics and an upbeat call to action. *'A mystic journey through a diverse selection of heavenly looped violins, warm percussion and insightful spoken word. There's never a dull moment on the disc.'* – Urbnet

DaZoque! (CD) by DaZoque!
'Urban Montreal meets a Slavic mountain village under a full moon.' Exquisite East European flavoured instrumentals by a string ensemble anchored by the core violin duo of Minda Bernstein and Nawrocki.
'Wedding music for anarchists. While they fiddle, sampled loops & electric guitars burn' – The Globe & Mail

MUSIC

Rhythm Activism, More Kick! (CD)
RA's 14th high-energy release, recorded live in Europe, inspiration for Nawrocki's book, The Anarchist & The Devil do Cabaret.
'Intelligent musical buffoonery' – Bruits, Paris
'Stunning & deeply moving' – Opscene, Amsterdam

Rhythm Activism, Blood and Mud (CD)
RA's captivating homage to the Zapatista rebellion in Chiapas, Mexico. Traces the roots. Nawrocki co-founded RA.
'Brilliant mixture of sound and words' – Magnet, Philadelphia
'Should be mandatory listening for members of Congress' – Option, L.A.

The Montreal Manhattan Project (CD)
Nawrocki's experimental jazz trio with Aaron Shragge & Greg Anderson Smith. A haunting potpourri of looped cello, viola and violin, with soaring trumpet and sparse, beautiful electronica.

SANN (CD)
Original, atmospheric, ambient creations. Highly imaginary, visual music with Chapman Stick Bass, bass, violin and viola. A duo of Nawrocki and Sylvain Auclair.

Order from Les Pages Noires:
www.nothingness.org/music/rhythm
Contact: rhythm@nothingness.org